AF487756

Everything English attract no interesting English

(Amidst Connections, Observations, and Reviews)

Pramod Kesav N

Notion Press

NOTION PRESS

India. Singapore. Malaysia.

Everything English attract no interesting English

Foreword

This book, Everything English attract no interesting English, amidst Connections, Observations, and Reviews is a technical book in English literature. It is also meant as a most basic form of learning styles in English literature where a few adages or paraphrases are taken and examined revealing the meaning and gist of aligned events and imagery.

Since it is written in a technical format, care is taken to go descriptive on most aspects that demand explanations.

Hope it is an easy read for all.

With best wishes to all,

Pramod Kesav N

(Payikkattu, Kalavamkodam, Cherthala, Alappuzha, Kerala, India)

Preface

Throughout this work, it is emphasized common metaphorical phrases in English and about the proponents of them from ages ago in England and the rest of the world, wield an influence on us as it affects literally the makeup of our own world whether English speaking or not, in a place, where it gathers certainly individualistic guilds acting as limiting approaches and explorations by us, the individuals.

However, throughout this work, what is emphasized and attempted is to second or support a stand of favouritism that goes in line with a melange of people breaking the racial wall of diversification by stretching away from puritan thoughts and by paving a way for lessening of class distinctions in the literary parlance.

Unless diverse thoughts and viewpoints are accepted, there is no go ahead for us as a human race, we hit stumbling blocks and remain in silos ultimately reducing our existence to a pot hole or a well, with no passer-by who may offer us a pail of water or a rope to get out of our current misery.

We as rightful owners of this planet is no lesser than an occupant of a dwell, on the other side of the globe and the discriminative treatments should end, by breaking chain, no matter whether we are a worker, an alien, or a resident in any country but law abiding everywhere in the world.

Once that acceptance as a person in a country is in place where the state guarantees all basic and fundamental rights and necessities, forced class distinctions may be averted upon persons if it does not hamper his fundamental existence in a state of his choosing and his beliefs.

If for some reason one does not like a state or a country, or may find their laws discriminating to oneself, one should then have full rights to choose stay or leave that country on one's own will. In order to get there, it is important that one learns what one can about their ways of life, their culture, their personalities, not to create havoc or mela in any of their setup but to try to adapt and adjust with them by gaining knowledge and in peaceful means.

It is hoped that my work: Everything English and works in English literature by very many authors like me may go a long way towards achieving that.

Hope you have a peaceful stay wherever you are!

Thanks!

Pramod Kesav N

(Author)

Table of Contents

Literals

and the literature that follows...

1

Everything English attract no interesting English

Everything English is undoubtedly a well sought out subject in Social Media, needless to say it had its peak viewership of 20 hits sometime in the beginning of the year 2020 and from then on, it is an average 1 hit an year.

So, this subject has not progressed as some of its creators may want it to, from growing from an absolute zero hit to say a few thousand or hundred hits a day.

That is when I realized that it indeed was not an interesting subject. What I was interested to see was what makes it a dull subject.

Everything English or any title as is suggested, I guess nobody wanted it, since it signifies only the Anglican way of life, remember the Anglican way of life is always with something or somebody, Anglo-Saxon, Anglo-Latin, Anglo-Indian. Maybe, that is what it is.

But I thought what the heck.

Now, I thought I will put some flavour into the cuisine, thought let me draft out the contents in a slightly different way for Everything English by picturizing it as what the English always wanted the world to look like for them.

That is when I started getting ideas.

I thought I would include the living styles and standards of native or mixed native groups in South America and Africa, include a documentary of their languages such as Creoles and Pidgins, included information about the Juka Language, about Creolized West Africa, in general about what the English inspired all around the globe with sadly nothing of their living styles reflected in any of that.

And that got it going.

However, I did not change the tile. I called the documentary or video as Everything English but it still did not attract anybody to the wellness of those much-curated content.

The story remained the same.

Less viewership.

It looked as though most viewers shunned the show.

Let us leave that part aside.

Finally, I realized in the Social Media, the videos under the title: Everything English is not going to make it. It by far remained as a set of fine and best variety documentary in the social media contents inviting no or little attention from the viewers.

Now, let us take a different viewpoint, as somebody seemed to have whispered "gloom", how accurate that is; it is not just about anybody's call but surely let us whisper and take a different perspective on the saying, Every cloud has a silver lining. By doing so we will try to describe some of the understanding after experiencing incidents that are foretold or personal and whether there lied a scope for hope, after going through with them.

Well, if in the social media, a documentary with title: Everything English did not fare well, and then so be it, let us firmly believe in the adage, that even the gloomiest outlook sometimes contains hopeful or consoling aspects.

David Rosse Locke who was the friend of Mark Twain and Josh Billings, was well known for his Nasby letters, alter ego: Petroleum V Nasby, where every political event including questions like whether slavery is in an accepted form in Bible in support of Confederates initiated a lot of talk even from the President of USA (Abraham Lincoln).

Despite the usages of semi-literate spellings or akin Bulter English elsewhere used by humourists of those times in the USA, he was well heard of as a Copperhead, in Struggles of "P (Petroleum). V. Nasby" when he told, there was a silver linen in every cloud.

More or less the same happened with P.T. Barnum when after his successful popularity with "Feejee" mermaid and being the beneficiary of the Lind mania, he felt there sure was cloud, as per the proverb, that has a silver lining, shortly after his investments in Jeremy Clock Company went bust in East Bridgeport, Connecticut, in the latter half of the nineteenth century.

It is also questionable to analyse whether the same feeling existed when one read the book, The Redundancy of Courage from Mo owe to its graphical rendition and not so comfortable ways of its descriptions

In the year 2002, The Spectator magazine at the centre of a political circus, engaged sensationalism in such a way that it prioritized it over journalistic integrity. It is said these overtures might have affected the magazine's credibility and, in a way, it led to diminishing role of media in shaping up political upheavals and narratives.

So, to recall, What just happened in the year 2002 for The Spectre magazine and Were there a silver lining to every cloud that emerged from there?

Let us see...

In 2002, The Spectator magazine, a publication which leans more conservative was in the middle of significant controversies. It questioned the magazine and its role of a purveyor of political sensationalism. In one of its episodes, believed to be funded by the conservative donor Richard Mellon Scaife investigated scandalous stories about Bill (former President of the USA) and Hillary Clinton. Later The Spectator faced criticism for its role in promoting conspiracy theories being orchestrated as part of a political circus. Since nothing turned out to be true, it created significant damage to the role of magazines, in general promoting political upheaval, and political narratives in US during the year 2002.

So, to recap, social media creativity like the documentary with title: Everything English may be a popular item or not with the viewers but that does not mean, we should have a shortage on documentaries or videos and as creators, one must stop worrying about how popular one gets with the content but rather on, how influencing one is, especially in gathering useful and convincing connections and show courage and attitude to venture out in rather unfamiliar territories.

2

Prepared to usage lead to formulaic phrases

In any forms of transaction, transparency is the key that one ought to maintain no matter what, whether one ends up in creating news that is sensational, or one who in the process may get into scurrilous situations prompting endless altercations on streets, and with the press, and ends up digging one's own hole, leading that one to realize the meanings of chasm, gorge, and what not.

Rather than be ready to face the ever-ending animosity of the spectators, many condescend an opinion, by supplementing evidences and in all their efforts in whatever form they write; there are references everywhere citing truths as may be approved by a panel, an authoritative body exercising truthful renditions in a certain region, field, subject which no matter what, is required to some extent, or degree.

However, what is increasingly seen is the validity of such thesis being constantly questioned, in an era of digital makeup, where it is one thing to go based on accepted truths, as it existed from when on, which is quite the right thing, as expressed in many of my previous works as opposed to bending the premises of an opinion so that it fits with a recently found wisdom.

Many a times, eloquent speakers lose their grip, and is seen to go opinionated beyond their comfort zone where a certain approach that they take is seen to be immediately contradictory to what they originally intended to accomplish, be it in a modern rendition of a tutelage or be it delivering the last rights of a famed but a framed accomplice.

Needless to add a perfect interpretation of a prefect-sense is not going to help anybody here rather than lead many to fit into a world of picture-perfect disillusions, quite often making its inhabitants immobile in a world of stillness, and the frozen landscape.

But speak, one sure needs to speak and must get into conversations but to what extent?

Normally, we as seasoned speakers of the English language, hate to see the usage of formulaic phrases like prepared to and not in a position to in normal conversations.

If you have not hated to use such phrases, for sure, Ernest Gowers did hate, especially when he was bombarded with official documents, this time, many in numbers of very many different varieties of documents. At that juncture, Gowers was never prepared to or be in a position to or may not see his way to defend something of nature archaic type of why certain argument that he said or stated is in a certain way, or from where an original thought arises in a certainty time frame spurring argumentative disclosures to his spectators...

Hence formulaic phrases should be used with caution as is given in the English text, The Complete Plain Words, especially when one refers against another's standpoint which goes into a conflict in reasoning behind one's belief systems, so on and so forth.

In political science, as a matter of usage of formulaic phrases, this type of directional planning results in a complete reversal of standpoints where one is seen to move from a certain decision to a set of directly opposing decisions in a split second.

As per Earnest Gower, whenever he condemns examples such as in his own usages of Formulaic phrases, he was neither prepared to disclose the source of information nor prepared to overlook any discrepancy resulting out of his English usage as though he only wants to blur the meaning of the word or usage, prepared to.

As per him, usual usages in English, like "prepared to" should be reserved for statements in which there is an element of preparation.

Hence, no questions are entertained to him, when he says I have read papers and am now prepared to hear your side of the story.

This is definitely followed in White Hall but still the meaning or gist of it, looms around the rest of the world.

In conclusion, hence it can be easily seen that, the way Ernest presents his way of an argumentative note flaps wings with GB Shaw when he says, I came here to place it before a body of persons of European distinction but not prepared to discuss it with an irresponsible English woman.

Besides attending to the reader's plight after making this statement, it is like getting prepared to listening to such statements, reminds us of an incident that occurred when the government was not prepared to fight for realistic exclusion zones for the British fisherman suggesting rethinking on the part of English think tanks.

They were no doubt were prompted in an out of league push to the extent that prompted authorities feign local ones prepared to remove bad English teachers from their immediate school zones.

Most understood this and agreed that from a Scottish perspective druids may work in their place but from a Finnish perspective folks definitely flap their wings, and the flocks safely sit on rocks.

The last line goes this much adding a lasting belief to some of them to be prepared and not leave us all to think in a more Fowler way, the original intent of the English usage "getting prepared to" is to say be willing or be dispossessed to do something.

In short, Action speaks more than words.

Now what action? And how loud it speaks? Where it is loudly spoken? And how loud it gets when in fact what speaks is the entire country? Yes, in most countries, in parliamentary democracy or in elected houses of democratic countries, it speaks, it speaks in such a manner that there definitely is action that follows. Yes, it is true. There in those elected houses if it speaks louder or not, action definitely speaks louder than words, and action, sure it follows the speech.

But all these speeches or most of it unless it is stricken down is part of parliamentary proceedings. In some countries, Hansard is the official record of parliamentary debates and is used in many democratically elected countries to document discussions in a more transparent way. It is always the written record of whatever is spoken by the members in the Parliament. It is an official document of these debates, which is very important and crucial for accountability and transparency in any form of democratic governance.

American Civil War

Apple of Gold in pictures of silver originated from Bible, particularly in Proverbs 25:11 which translated roughly as "A Word fitly spoken is like apples of Gold in pictures of silver.".

However, during the American Civil War, this phrase gained a very specific and powerful meaning because of its use by the President of the USA, Abraham Lincoln.

Lincoln's use of this phrase was first taken mention of in his work (1864) in a private note titled, "Fragment on the Constitution and Union". There, Abraham Lincoln used this verse from the Bible to explain his view of what existed as a relationship between the Constitution, Union, and the principle of liberty.

There the simile was on Union and Constitution being picture of silver, and fitly spoken which was an apple of gold. He also meant by saying apple of gold upheld the principle of liberty and equality and conveyed the idea that all men are created equal which remained the core moral truth, which is again, the apple of gold. This core principle was to be supported in pictures of silver which were the constitution and the union and not the Confederates.

Hence, during civil war, this metaphor existed and was used as an argument to support the very existence of Union and Constitution to preserve liberty, equality and not any protection to slavery. It also provided moral support wherever required even if it meant clarity for the Civil war efforts that the Union was engaged in with the Confederates. However, there was a common call which were believed to be in existence during then amongst the Union, the fight with the Confederates were to protect not just the Union but also human equality at heart.

During that time, Andrew McFarland Davis who was a prominent scholar published a collection of colonial currency reprints titled Colonial Currency Reprints of 1682 till 1751 (published by Prince Society). This comprehensive overview of the currency system that were used in American colonies gave a significant knowhow of how those currencies were used, to the people living in the liberated or more advanced Union states.

More over during that time, Embargo Act of 1807 was passed in the United States Congress which was a general trade embargo on all foreign nations representing an escalation of attempts by Britain, and to stop imprisonment of American sailors and to respect American sovereignty. Remember, it is in the same year that Britain passed the Slaves Trade Act (Abolishing) prohibiting Atlantic slave trade in the British Empire which may have included what remained of British North America (mostly Canadian provinces).

So, it can be assumed that internal trade that was in existence in the United States during 1807 was really difficult and the traders had a very difficult time getting resources to foster an average means of living.

In the American colonies, this meant, there was heavy demand for Colonial Currency Reprints of 1682 till 1751.

However, after 1863, Abraham Lincoln played a key role in abolishing slavery in the United States but as was told, it only happened in stages. In his Emancipation Proclamation Lincoln declared that all enslaved people in the states which were Confederate states shall then and will be forever free.

Abraham Lincoln also had reiterated a call that is said to be from the Confederates, asking for measures or rather "Give us the measures and you take the men" which may be interpreted as political measures to help slaves be free or give cloth measurements of garments for slave men in the Confederate states so that the Confederates be right out of the Confederate states.

So, it was, may be rather unpleasant for Confederates to bear the consequences of them being unlawful in the Confederate states, after slavery was abolished there, that prompted an acute call from them (Confederates) as was given in the Abraham Lincoln's Works (1953).

Now those Confederate men surely must have moved to the Union states from the Confederate states and may have raised families in the Union states, which may have prompted writers like Morna Stuart (1939), who was a British writer and a playwright to have published on her themes of justice, guilt and complexity of emotions which left those living to grapple with the consequence of their actions.

Now, why should writers like Morna Stuart feel guilty amidst a plethora of emotions?

It is because she or writers like her might have known about the state of affairs of some of the American women who were in conjugal arrangements with some of the questionable characters from the Confederate states.

Hence, it can be concluded that these American women had a hard time adjusting to their harsh realities, in the beginning of the twentieth century, and during early 1930s to 1940s to have left with no option but to face the grunt of their reality by facing all the challenging experiences both in the personal front and professional front, in the difficult years after the American civil war and the Great Depression (1930s), let alone any liberation attempts in many forms of woman empowerment seemed to have happened during then, after the conclusion of the World wars in the twentieth century.

This expression of Morna, also vibrates with the idea that action speaks louder than words. Various thinkers also had expressed it during that time just like what Morna did.

In summary, Morna Stuart's works in the year 1939 in titles: Dead Men sing no songs and the Traitor's Gate (play) offer an examination that is so profound of how the past, especially those actions by her or her acquaintances that cannot be undone, continue to influence the present.

3

Beg your pardon?

Beg your pardon? Are there more questions? The assemble session is in progress in the sixties memorabilia and my friend Twain is interrogated now as we speak.

Excerpts?

Interrogator: Are you a goat?

Mark Twain: "Wazz". This is indicative of a good quality leather glove that was worn which is absolutely all-weather proof and needed no introduction.

Interrogator: Then, Are you a goat who frequently visits inns where there are already rumours that you hath the best form of breakfast in casseroles?

Mark Twain: Breakfast is a matter, of fact a very delicious meal for a brisk rider who is not a Cannibal and who frequently visits Missouri in the US. It is a place that gives a sigh of relief too when there and when there to feed from a casserole.

Interrogator: Beg the pardon, I meant beg the question? You keep disapproving all good decisions that I am about to take. Do you think it is righteous on your part to keep doing it?

Mark Twain: It may not be righteous but it sure gives enough room to ask for more rights, like Individual rights, Group conscience, social freedom, and what not?

Interrogator: So, you are adamant in going ahead with reinstating night rider Lily as the new state flower?

Mark Twain: Well, if it gives closure to some of the recommendations that you had already raised, besides social freedom is to be enjoyed by all.

Interrogator: Social freedom, are you or do you habitually do clap trap?

Mark Twain: No clap trap or none so whatsoever of what may be reminiscent of when it originally started way back in 1820. As a member of the ensemble (political drama), which thyself is not, I should say all what most leaders do is to impress the constituents but when it comes to the assemble podium, the reader still insists the member to speak rather than mumble on an important question as it relates to the formation of something like a state?

And again, there, do not connect the Missouri questions with the Maastricht treaty in the present time as Mr. Major did? Because the more you do the more you turn yourself into a bum and not a bunkum.

So, does that mean I am chained and detained by the authorities goes a bemused Twain now who still thinks he was detained by the authorities on behalf of those authors who stood for sentimental and emotional writing, A Moralist story?

This might have been what were to be expected as a response from my friend Twain also, whose alter ego: Mark Twain reflected well with a profound realist approach, a perfect spokesperson of Literary Realism.

It is well known reality for sure where Mark Twain stood in the US in the late nineteenth century along with his counterparts in the UK, George Eliot, Charles Dickens, Thomas Hardy who all had one thing in common; about the present situation, the current predicament; of what those revered people set themselves against solving common man's problems, issues, and day to day chant and nothing else.

Particularly it should be kept in mind, of what Across Europe (another work) saw which is, nothing short of strengthening of Literary Realism movements meant for ordinary people which goes without a question to say this much, that it overshadowed Kingsley's more sentimental, emotional or moralist writing.

So, Charles Kingsley a British writer, theologian and social reformer was also a significant figure in the Victorian era who may have wanted authorities to move against Mark Twain during those days at least in a more philosophical way. Shocking, isn't it?

Though true or not, such was the animosity kept by these literary characters that animated hatred, vengeance and class play and sometimes revenge was written all over in most of the argumentative literature that each of them used to come out with, and presented as in seemingly evident disclosures, as in Cornhill magazine.

But some more questions need to be answered.

Why should a Twain be so profoundly fond of the Night rider Lily that may have thwarted Kingsley to call the devil and then their so-called weaker links.

Did he anticipate that the chain that was put on Twain or that was used to detain Twain break at a weaker link or did he want the full story of the numerous but weakest links from that era.

Yes, the western world always worked in a certain way.

They constantly avoided the weak, weaker, or the weakest links not necessarily in that order and retained only the strong, stronger, and strongest definitely not in that order to lead the way, no matter what reality the strongest believed in and lived, due more from their actions and adventures, gifting sometimes the most picture-perfect world as a direct dementia out of God's blessings.

Throughout the writing and works of Leslie Stephen in the 1860s, who was a Victorian era editor of the Cornhill magazine, some thoughts reflect well off from his work: Times on the American war, a historical study or a melancholy to strike off the chain which is no stronger than its weakest link.

The part of his letters featuring the sorry state of affairs depicted in black and white in the numerous ongoing conversations between Sum, Greedy, Sewards in section: Tragedy of Abraham Lincoln, where very many, who were acting spectators were made to think in the western world of the plight the army in the Union states of US and of what remains of their Roman army, mockingly the chained slaves where the authorities seemed to break the chain of slavery, and of where it needs to be broken, and its cruel enactments of the weakest links being broken epitomizing accounts of cruelty, in essence resulting in challenging circumstances rendering challenged and weaker sections of the slave society that we must cite with.

Yes, it is true Leslie Stephen though sympathetic with the subject: Abolishing of slavery is equally adamant of what sort of opportunities exist for the fighting men, when the abolishing initiatives are seen in the light of suffering pendants and the suffocating rich on the contrary, reminiscent of the physically challenged weaker sections of their society from the more recently freed slaves.

The chain is broken at the weakest link and sure the Union states of the US have a lot of physically and mentally challenged people, but the horrible stories should come out and nobody likes to take a listen or listen to them.

For them abolishing of slavery meant there existed more stronger men on their side who have successfully broken the chains of slavery, but nobody wants to listen to the weaker ones amongst them, they are long being forgotten to the pages of a minimum historical flap, a marginalized society.

Evident from Leslie Stephen's own writing when he quotes, "If you show how admirably the last few were united, many forget to test the security, and there again..., parts kept out of sight suggesting everything is evident, and in the west most all want the physically strong to lead, let alone, only the physically strong survive. The perfect saying, Survival of the physically fittest.

<u>Deregulation and smaller governments</u>
During 1980 throughout the United States, the Executive franchise of the government backed by the general public felt the frustration inherent in bloated bureaucracies both at the government level and in the corporate world.

A few years later during 1986, a management model: Peter Pyramid started gaining ground with the Ronald Reagan era administration so much so that its significance grew deeper with the Ronald Reagan bureaucrats when all started asking whether one ever gets the point, the point being Peter's 1986 book: The Peter Pyramid.

It was understood that in several government positions the longer the chain of delegation, the more the presence of weak links.

Since it was the United States government, weak links were blamed to be the cause of break in communications and any distortions that may have caused information loss, may have led the American president, Ronald Reagan resort to smaller government and Deregulation that went in line with Peter's satirical critique of the government's hierarchical inefficiency.

Alongside changes in the public administration, the line of action in the government's various institutions give way to a cultural reflection where the Peter Pyramid tapped into broader concerns about authority, meritocracy, and systemic failures in education, healthcare, military and in various corporations.

It was later found out that hierarchical systems can sabotage effectiveness and give way to political and management manoeuvrability extending the original Peter Principles in federated and federal employment positions.

Organizational efficiency and COP21

Organizational efficiency in precise military installations in harsh weather conditions rely on the sound upkeep of all of its members where there is an unsaid danger that arises when even one team member is careless or loses their nerve especially in high stakes combat situations.

Now how relevant any discussions on organizational efficiency outside military installations is evident when one sees the success rate of what an original conference on climate change is; like what was in store in the year 2015 with COP21, UN Climate change in Paris yielded which was attended by leaders from 147 nations is questionable, what you see is its aims partially fulfilled and what is final was not entirely keeping the Global warming level below 2° centigrade.

A lot of things were at stake.

On June 18th, 2015, Pope Francis blamed human selfishness for the Global warming that happened across the world.

Years later, it was observed that the colder icy exteriors of South America and the Antarctica melted to a level where they started experiencing tropical like climate within a reasonable reach of Maitri and Bharati, both Indian research stations in Antarctica.

4

Clean Energy Initiatives and the Carbon Emission Standards

It is imperative that the Carbon emissions be codified in such a manner that makes the system responsible, to give it a measurement yardstick or score, with which the Carbon Emissions are measured in one region in relation to the emission standards of other regions.

In the European continent, it is said that the Carbon emissions are really in a very alarming level, that in Europe, Industrial expansion is a near impossibility, more pointing fingers at reducing the Industrial expansion and cut down on the Manufacturing and Industrial output owe more due to these Carbon Emissions.

Hence, in the western world, it is a fact that they must reduce Carbon emissions or make sure depletion of Carbon dioxide is a reality, that the Carbon Emissions are reduced by planting more trees in their Industrial vicinity and give back the life line by taking away Carbon dioxide presence in their atmosphere.

Now, these measures are really not acceptable in countries like Denmark, where any cut down on their industrial real estate might really affect the economics of those countries.

Hence, the Western Industries (industries in the Western countries) or in particular the European industries have spearheaded motions in their political system, where by, the stance taken, is in attempting to increase the forest area in tropical countries like India or Brazil, and by afforestation, whereby the depletion of carbon dioxide (due to Europe's carbon emissions) is accounted for and the participating countries (developing and underdeveloped) compensated by means of what is called Carbon Credits or any fund that may emerge out of Red Funds.

Before we explain on this topic any further, let us examine what are Carbon Credits and what is Red Fund, which are mostly driven by Western interests.

Carbon Credits:
Carbon emissions in the western world in particular in European countries have reached alarming levels and is recommended by international bodies, that the European countries reduce the industrial assets so that depletion of CO_2 from the atmosphere may take place and the pollutants from industries are reduced to minimum levels.

On the other hand, what the European industries are vouching at, is Carbon Credits, whereby if there is an industrial attempt to reduce the carbon footprint of existing or future system by a metric, that metric can be sold for a sum to particular industry in any country in the world so that their carbon emission by that metric is justified and allowed in the present scenario.

For instance, if a Solar Panel manufacturer in India, creates Solar panels and sells let us say x units in the Indian Market, and gains y units of Carbon Credit; those Carbon credits so obtained by the Solar Panel manufacturer in India can be sold in India or anywhere in the world at a price, so that the acquirer industry of the Carbon Credit anywhere in the world can in other words go on with Carbon emissions stipulated by the metric of Carbon Credit which is actually acquired by virtue of that sale.

So, this Carbon Credit business is a huge business all around the world, and there are many players in the global market, in stock exchanges in certain countries etc. We won't delve deep into the specifics of that business but what is important is that, there is a mechanism available to industries in the western world where their Carbon emissions may be justified merely by acquiring the Carbon credits from the rest of the world.

Now let us see what are Red Funds.

Red funds on the other hand is money pooled in by the Western world, notably, European countries and countries like USA and the UK, whereby they distribute this money through international bodies like the UNDP (United Nations Development Programme) to countries that are developing and underdeveloped urging them to grow forests or attempt afforestation so that a better Carbon footprint exist in an overall global scenario, whereby the Western world's industrial emissions get justified and the so called virtuous deeds inspire afforestation in the developing world.

Remember, any attempts of afforestation or increasing the forest area in the developing world come at an expense to the developing world, of that of displacement of existing establishments (Family units) in the so-called areas which were once upon a time, forest.

Remember also that the sole beneficiary of measures like the Red Fund or Carbon Credit is the Western industries in particular the European industries and in one way they are pushing for the creation of forests in the tropical countries (Countries like India, Brazil, and continents like Africa) so that the Carbon Emissions which is the responsibility of the Western industry is justified, giving rise to local laws which forces normal people to be forced to relocate from the present habitats.

It is also interesting to see, if any good practice will be followed in the Western world so that the scepticism is kept out by strengthening the preposterous energy equations to go in sync with the business activities sprawling a locality or area in the West in particular in European countries.

In short, the bottom line remains, and can be stated that the business should quantify the energy requirements, and assess the Carbon emission standards suitable for a certain environment around which they operate and demand Carbon Credits from Vendor companies of Green energy so that business goes as usual and the environment is deeply unimpacted.

Green Hydrogen Refuelling

With the advent of the National Hydrogen Mission, there is a huge drive for Alternate fuel based on Renewable Energy, more popularly Green Hydrogen based schematics, with its subjects that are still in an innovation stage from an effective cost perspective, transportation, and dispensation efforts.

This article draws the bare basic logistics of the Future Green Hydrogen based Refuelling stations.

With the introduction of Toyota Mirai Hydrogen powered vehicle, the tank capacity of the Toyota Mirai is set at 5.5 kg of Hydrogen.

One Kilo of Green Hydrogen gives roughly 107 Kilometres in this car, where it is priced currently between Rs. 300 to Rs. 400 (Grey Hydrogen) and may be frugally affordable than, the other variant of Hydrogen (Green Hydrogen).

However, it is definitely set to improve due to increased efforts and money spent in this area and also, it is said that one kilogram of Green Hydrogen has the same energy capacity as 1 Gallon (3.2 kilogram) of Gasoline.

The normal or regular tanker truck that transports Green Hydrogen typically can haul 600 kilogram of Green

Hydrogen which is 14 times lesser than when what is hauled when it is Gasoline.

Hydrogen can then get stored in Type III or Type IV containers or be stored in Solid State Storage (made of Metal and Complex Hydrides) or in the form of Liquid Hydride Storage.

IH2A recommends uniform sets of Bharat H2 Standards for H2 storage, for its transportation, and its dispensation.

Usually, Green Hydrogen can get transported in a pressurized gaseous form or as a cryogenic liquid, also can be transported in a chemical precursor form such as Lithium, Sodium Metal, or Chemical Hydrides.

For the prices to come down of that of Green Hydrogen, Electricity cost should be brought down of Renewable Energy (Solar or Wind power) as well as the cost of Electrolysers should also be brought down.

Enapter, who is a European leader in the manufacture of Electrolyser is working towards bringing down the cost of Electrolysers to 1000 to 2000 EURO for 2.4 KW.

Here, Cost of renewable energy need to be lower for Green Hydrogen to be below 4 per Kilowatt to be in competing terms with Grey Hydrogen.

Overall, the logistics work is undertaken by many, but time will prove how cost effective and affordable the Green Hydrogen refuelling stations are, to the common public.

Roads in England

In Spectator magazine in the year 2012, there was an article which detailed Rome's control over the empire's landscape and popular beginnings and endings were detailed or could very well be imagined after going through with that anecdote.

To say the least all roads lead to Rome. In ancient times, what bothered the inhabitants in the hamlets of the Roman empire is surely the galloping sounds made by the Roman soldiers. For ways and means advances, these soldiers might have collected taxes for occupancy, land, and their demand for allegiance may have given nightmares to horrified countrymen of the settlements in the Roman empire.

That is, when we say all roads lead to Rome and centuries later someone's interest on the roads in England.

Huxley and an Individual in Animal Kingdom

In 1912 Huxley came out with a work, Individual in Animal Kingdom and proclaimed to the world in quote: Even animal individuality (horses) throws a ray (of hope) on human problems.

His work definitely may have pondered well on primitive habits of humans that a man gets accustomed with as well as animal like behaviour he or she may experience, when they adjust and leans on the basis of a premises drawn to contain primitive and primate behaviour in a unique form, quite distinct from the human form. He or the Man then thinks about the ray of hope and an exit out of human problems that may have bothered him until then or well before willingly giving up on his human persona, an easy alteration of emotional forms to an inhuman conscience.

The Individual in the Animal Kingdom is a seminal work by Julian S Huxley, which was first published in the year 1912. In this work, Huxley goes explorative over the concept of individuality in animal kingdom but within the animal kingdom, analysing the evolutionary science which aided the advancement of life's complexity from the viewpoint of organizations, and organizational behaviour.

His approach mostly Darwinian carefully draws a contrast between functional hierarchies and integrated forms within organisms, and loosely defined ecological communities which are in the premises of organismal ecology to the extent of no-organismal. Remember again, about what these beasts share with the humans? It is the road ahead.

<u>William Black and The Strange Adventures of a Phaeton</u>

The Strange Adventures of a Phaeton by William Black is a Victorian era novel which was published in the year 1870. This story features a group of British travellers on a journey which may be leisurely through Europe on a horse-drawn carriage or a phaeton, where the route includes some locations and locale, picturesque, offers a blend of social commentaries and travelogue.

La Fontaine's fables by R. Thompson

Now comes the question from an oblique corner asking for La Fontaine and on the roads that he most travelled as per the English translations of La Fontaine's Fables by Robert Thompson.

To which one should go more like this.

LaFontaine did not travel much, he feared travelling extensively but his vivid imaginations put him as the best travelogue writer during those times. He was of the opinion that all roads looked alike or are alike and goes towards Rome to conduct Rome. He may also have been fascinated in vivid imaginations by the ancient but powerful Roman infantry during those times.

In 1806, Robert Thompson translated the work Fables of Jean de La Fontaine. These translations were so effective that its sole aim was to make La Fontaine's works accessible to the English-speaking world.

Jean de La Fontaine who lived in the time period, 1621 to 1695 was a French poet who was well known for his fables which drew inspiration from Aesop, Eastern tales, and literature that were mostly classical genre. While La Fontaine himself was not much of a traveller, cultural influence was inherent in his works indicating his exposure to philosophies and diverse stories through intellectual and literature circles.

It incorporated characters and settings from different parts of the world, from rural France, Orient, and ancient Greece and this diversity made La Fontaine's work well read, engaged with narratives that were global with commentaries on human nature and society.

The narratives in these fables, though fictional mirrored the experiences of individuals who ventured out beyond their family surroundings encountering different challenges, and cultures.

These stories of his in Fables resonate with the wider audience because the broader human experience is what is thrown open to all in matters of exploration and the meaningful quest.

Geoffrey Chaucer and Astrolabe

To start, let us try to see the roads a Geoffrey Chaucer took, along with his Astrolabe in 1391, when he was on a mission to go to Rome. Now, why should he go, is his own business, maybe he held several royal appointments with the Clerk of the King's works, he may have wanted to meet the Justice of the Peace, or maybe he may have wanted to visit the Royal Envoy of the Roman empire.

In the early 1390s, he seemed to have faded away from all the courtly records but scholars still speculate that he may been the chosen one to be sent on a mission to the papal court, since Rome was the centre of diplomacy, royal interest, and church politics.

Now for the benefit of those who may have skipped a few of the literature classes, a short biography on Geoffrey Chaucer. He was the best known author of The Canterbury Tales, he also was not just a poet but a bureaucrat, diplomat, and a courtier.

In the year, 1391, he was believed to have been taking care of the Royal business which may have included a mission to Rome, though no substantive evidences lie for the time being for now.

Around the same time, he wrote the Treatise on the Astrolabe for the benefit of his son, Lodowick or Little Lewis, who was at that time ten years old, Chaucer was also commemorated as the person, who wrote the first known work of scientific instructions in English.

Again, to reiterate, All roads lead to Rome.

So, what roads might a Chaucer have taken to Rome in the year 1391?

There lies no concrete evidence that Chaucer took his family members to Rome or that Little Lewis existed beyond the treatise which was given to him.

That is because The Treatise on the Astrolabe is considered a more scientific journal and not a travelogue or a record of a travel or journey which Chaucer undertook.

But one should really imagine, to get a first-hand look at the road or route Chaucer took when on a trip to Rome in the year 1391.

Remember for a person of Chaucer's calibre, he had the option to choose one of, known medieval travel routes, or he may have chosen a pilgrimage path, or more simply, he may have travelled in a trade or a royal diplomatic route.

Let us for our own interest break the route which a Chaucer might have taken from London to Rome in the year 1391.

The first part says, he may have travelled from London to Dover, and then from Dover to Calais or Wissant by boat, and from overland through France, which may have taken him from Calais through Arras to Paris, and from then on continue south until he reached Lyon and then he may have continued through the Alps passing Mont Cenis Pass.

Mont Cenis Pass was said to be a dangerous path, especially in winter, where most of it was supposedly used by Pilgrims, Merchants, or clergies, where there were a lot of Monasteries on both sides of the road that led to Northern Italy which gave shelter to the travellers.

Once in Northern Italy, he may have travelled through the Alps, that is right from Turin, through Milan and all the way to Siena and then Rome.

Great, so he is in Rome now.

Could he have used astrolabe during his stays in Rome, in the Roman empire?

Possibly, he may have used astrolabe in Rome while in the Roman empire because he might have liked the experience of measuring stars, navigate by the heavens and he may have been in particular a person with deep knowledge on timekeeping, religious observance, and the astronomy. So, it makes sense.

He may have taken the astrolabe with him.

Now, could we know what an astrolabe is, the kind of instrument, which a Chaucer may have used in Rome, while in the Roman empire.

Yes, absolutely, one could very well elaborate a lot on the astrolabe, which is a scientific instrument of the medieval world used in astronomy, timekeeping, astrology, and navigation.

It also had metallic plates which were meant for its working in several and severe altitudes which held all the other components of that equipment. It also had optionally an Alidade, which is a ruler on the back of that instrument to measure altitude above the horizon.

Even though an Astrolabe is an instrument used by followers of Islam, it was also used in many Jewish and Christian cultures and is considered an early form of a portable science. This instrument by its use in Europe, gave way to later instruments like the sextant, and planisphere.

This instrument, astrolabe was beautifully crafted and often was considered a work of art with its bronze engraving, and beautiful calligraphy written all over.

Roads in England

Roads in England form a well-developed and an extensive network and plays a role which is crucial in the transportation of goods and commerce activities.

England's roads are classified as Motorways or M roads which are high speed roads for long distance travel and heavy traffic, A roads or minor roads that connect cities and large town, B roads that are secondary roads that link smaller towns and local areas, which have less traffic and are a lot narrower.

There also exist unclassified roads that serve in local and urban areas and include rural roads and residential streets.

London cabbies

London cabbies give a ride to its customers through the streets of London and they are considered an out of league group of drivers who has the knowledge of London, and their requirement is nothing short of memorizing every street, route, and landmark, within a six-mile radius from the centre of London, which is nothing but the landmark, Charing Cross.

This would mean they are supposed to know by-heart knowledge over 25,000 streets, thousands of points of interest, hospitals, pubs, parks, government buildings, embassies, etc.

Understanding how to navigate London through the fastest, most efficient routes without relying on GPS is solely the work of a London cabbie.

Hence, The Knowledge is one of the most difficult and respected taxi driver tests in the world and it trains and examines London black cab drivers by conducting of various tests so that they are licensed to drive in London.

Now how can one learn and pass the test?

Trainees spend three to four years preparing for The Knowledge. Some may use motor scooter rides to know better the streets, some may use Blue Book runs which is a set of standard 320 routes covering major parts of the city and some may even use flash card, maps, and what not.

The process tests not just geography but it is deeper than that, in content, tests mental maps and navigation which is more strategical.

It is not uncommon for students of the London Cabbie test, The Knowledge, to cover or ride tens of thousands of miles on scooters to get familiar with the area.

The dropout rate is generally higher and fewer people are now a days take the London Cabbie test, The Knowledge due to rise in Rideshare apps, etc.

As one cabbie may put it, "You can drop me blindfolded in any part of London, and I will tell you how to get to the Ritz, three pubs on the way, and the best shortcut when Oxford street is jammed".

<u>London Cabbie Stories</u>

London cabbies or London cab drivers especially the ones who drives the iconic black cabs, have the most varied stories which are rich in content as you may hear them similar on streets of any major city in the world. When you hear London cabbie stories, you experience and reflect the heart of London life, often laced with a sharp eye for people, their humour and grit.

Here it is presented an overview of some of the stories may be two stories from London cabbies they whole heartedly shared and every time one hears it, one gets inspired.

<u>The knowledge of the Lost Poet</u>

"You never really get lost in London, not if you're behind the wheel of a black cab.", said Dave who was a cabbie of 25 years old. He was referring to The Knowledge – the legendary and one of the most difficult cabbie tests which must be passed by the London cabbie in order to become cab drivers, memorizing 25,000 street and 20,000 landmarks.

One day when it was raining, or more so, in a rainy day, he picked up a quiet man with a thick notebook who did not speak much but when they passed through Bloomsbury, the passenger asked Dave to slow down. This corner, said the passenger, Virginia Wolf used to walk here, he told Dave.

Intrigued, Dave listened as the man recited poetry until when they reached Hampstead Heath.

Before stepping out, the man said, "You've probably got a hundred routes in your head. I just needed one. Then he handed Dave a slip of paper with a poem that was so original that Dave decided to tuck it behind his meter (in the car) to this day.

In afterthought, one may imagine that the poet whom Dave was referring to, may have been Julian Bell, son of Viriginia Woolf's sister, Venessa Bell and her husband Clive Bell. He was a member of Bloomsbury Group and lived in close proximity to V Woolf's residence in London. He was born in the year 1908 and tragically died in the year 1937 in Spanish Civil war.

Another person who may come in vivid imagination may be Charlotte Mew, a poet, Hilda Doolittle an American born Imagist or may even be Leigh Hunt (1784-1859), a prominent English critic, essayist, and poet.

One can also imagine that person to be the notable poet, D.H. Lawrence or Joan Adeney Easdale (1913-1988). Anyway, they all are immortal!

<u>Royal Fare, Regular Guy</u>

Mick, another old timer, once had a rider and he found it difficult to believe, which was a last-minute pickup from Savoy. A well-dressed man wanted to hire the cab to go to Buckingham Palace. Not a tourist, not a tourist, said Mick when he recalled the incident.

On arrival, the guards waved them through without a word.

Turns out, it was Prince Harry incognito, wanting to avoid the press after a charity event.

Mick goes beyond words even these days and could not be happier, whenever he tries to explain or recites the story.

7

What is cooking, Mrs. Murray?

An ambition is what gets one to go ahead, explore many different things in life, experiment with ideas and then spring out with the best form or possible form, which is the practical attribution of ideation to the practical side, in the field of engineering, the best form appears, emancipates in certainly some of the engineering applications in the field of civil, mechanical, and electrical engineering, that the designer who is its original conceiver, an owner in PTA (Patent, Trade Mark) terminology, better known as a Professional Engineer who is the conceiver of engineering ideas make it work, which would change, who knows the entire world around them.

In other words, for anybody who is a creator to work meaningfully in any corporeal setup (physical or materialistic or tangible or concrete), they are supposed to be first explorers of the world, with an acute sense of its dynamics, and relate the physical, metaphysical nature of its environment around them both physical and intangible to engineering principles and come out with a practical application, be it a model to harness energy, or be it to invent machines that would revolutionize the entire world.

Now to reach that goal, we know it takes a lot of effort assuming there exists opportunities, luck, and determination on the part of the engineering faculty to come out with a precise and clear-cut goal in contributing to nation's development efforts, be it infrastructure development, scientific advancements, advancements in transportation, space travel, defence systems, etc.

Our own country, India is also in a development trajectory, and we are now proud that we are poised for advancements in certainly science & technology, infrastructure development initiatives are there everywhere resulting in better roads, bridges, communication paraphernalia as well, in space-based technologies.

And when we are at that juncture where we are partly enjoying the advancements, Mrs Murray again does the trick. It was as if she let go loose a pack of hyena from her shelter, across continents now starts to bother innocent pedestrians on the walkway and the hyena is all set to attack them.

The pack (of hyena) does not stop there.

They are running everywhere with an intent to maul and be the initiator of a vicious dog attack and they do not differentiate whether it is a person, a moving vehicle, or a metal rod. They are running loose everywhere and are biting into everything on their way.

The last bite from us should be on fencing homes so that we safeguard our family, our friends and that may include any efforts as civilians, be it erecting fence around homes or the highways.

Civilians erecting fences around highways? Yes?

Infrastructure development is in fact..., that is another big question.

So, please think about it?

8

Transforming Cashmere Universe in the Robotic Literature

A universe once inhabited by Nymphs and Arcadians where the inhabitants accommodate the changing political landscape, accepts now the disappearance of royal orders in place gets accustomed with Public Scrolls and the Pessimistic Riddles.

The intent is what exists in, Cashmere universe that is severally depicted, the power centres splintered between power shareholders called Yeomen and Scarecrows, promise a ride to Pembroke's Arcadia if one ever wins the Preservation rights.

This is not done exactly by wars but is done with the help of scrolls and riddles; the best wit always gets accommodated among the burgeoning hierarchies in an abundance of wisdom in the Utopian lands of the Cashmere Universe!

Once accepted in the new universe, the inhabitants can become utopians, bohemians, dominion-dwellers, honour-thieves and devotionals and rest assured, they will be taken care of in every respect by the Neo Arcadian Government. The Neo-Arcadia is the name of the sprawling business dominion in the post-apocalyptic world of Mega Zero

Series men where it is said that many centuries ago saw humans and Reploids (author: Stephen King) live together side by side peacefully and harmoniously.

However there existed still Mavericks and the Cunning among them, who may reveal a plot which can put the inhabitants into a state of mind of that of the Zombies, only to be extradited to the furlong colder interiors of the Alaskan-Arcadia.

The second city of the Cashmere Universe is known by the name of Gallifrey and this city is famous for Apothecary services rendered immediately to the suffering pendants and the suffocating time lords of the Opportunistic lots and their communions of those larks that admire an attention.

Remember, Gallifrey is also the name of the planet that is the home world of Time Lords which is a fictional race, from Doctor Who is a British television series. It is a planet of immense power and ancient history, serving as a central location in the show's narrative.

A larger area in the Cashmere Universe is pastoral and there always used to be in existence a peaceful harmony between the inhabitants and the nature, idealistic in approaches that reminded everybody of their God Theo-criticism and of his lasting influence.

For those who liked the alternate ways of life, there always was in existence Eclogues and Monuments to take refuge in and for celebrating life in the Pastures following the Theo-criticism's ideals and mythologies.

Amongst its many inhabitants this belief of the prophecy is so strong that Alfius (Latin name) remains the saviour and the leading alter ego for all who gets protected from Zombies and from the unconventional.

Near the Tower of London

The Yeomen of the Guards also, The Merryman and his Maid is a Savoy opera by Gilbert and Sullivan, performed first at the Savoy theatre on October 3rd,1888 in London.

During the 18th century is where the opera is set in a palace or mansion, Tower of London, where the story revolves around Colonel Fairfax, a scientist and soldier wrongfully sentenced to death for sorcery. To prevent his estate being passed to his cousin, Fairfax gets into a secret arrangement of marriage with Elsie Maynard, a strolling singer. The marriage is so intended that it makes her a widow within one hour of getting married, securing his estate for her benefit. However, Fairfax's escape plan leads to complications and the story from whence, goes on and on...

Regarded as Arthur Sullivan's finest, Gilbert scores with some undulating mockery tips in the Yeomen of the Guard opera which is set against the backdrop of the Tower of London. The character Sir Richard Cholmondeley is also based on a real-life historical figure but for now let us pass all of it.

However, what is in our interest is the mockery that remains, the mockery on institutions, well the mockery on companies...

Certainly, the jokes and satire this time is well pointed towards the Company, a limited liability company or is it the company a wise man keeps?

Some jibes, we will go through, quote: "A company, you say? Ha! 'Limited liability'—the greatest disguise since Lady Veronne hid her debts in a duchess's wig! The officers dine in velvet while the creditors chew parchment!"

"Observe how the LLC struts, all pomp and protection! 'Tis not a man, nor a woman, nor even a beast—but a legal ghost that drinks champagne and cannot be arrested!"

"'Pierce the corporate veil!' cries the debtor—but alas, the veil is stitched of gold filings and lawyer's teeth."

"I once duelled a man for honour. Now, I duel subsidiaries for indemnity clauses. The sword is dull; the contracts endless!"

Oh, to be a company! Immortal, invisible, taxed like a whisper and blamed like a shadow!", unquote: over.

Now the questions that we may ask mainly since it was the beginning of the twentieth century is; Were the unsaid jibes at the Company, strike discord at companies like English (British) East India Company or the British East India Company that stopped operations by then. As told; Was it a company a wise men kept for all he knows in a limited liability concern?

As for the play, Merryman and his maid always leave someone broken hearted, sometimes it is a Jack and other times it is a Major John.

At the beginning, reuniting Elsie and Fairfax is what got it moving for the Savoy Opera but in Utopia Limited, it opened mockery where most of it mocked the companionship and pacifism, the real essentials in Limited Companies.

Now the liability, think about it, think about Utopia Limited, after all, it was not the length of the red carpet that was the obvious point of contention but where it was laid settled the start of another mockery, a drama, on LLC.

What Gilbert might have thought apart from the comic rendition of the fictitious character in everyone is the alter-ego, which kept on attaining heights despite its original proprietor begging on streets with folded arms, palms and what not to make ends meet.

Also now, Mona Tessa (a cloth pattern) walks on with girt gown with or without help from a Maria Monaci Gallenga (1880–1944) who was an Italian textile and fashion designer, while walking between two positions, making decisions from a gamut of choices or ideas and let us hope it pays way to staunch idealism and lasting peace which is not one thing or the other, gist is the verb and not proverb "gird", where girt remains past participle form of girded.

<u>Hold your tongue, ...</u>
Hold your tongue, a mockery on Corporation it seems!

Corporations have neither soul to be damned nor bodies to be punished. A large corporation unlike a private individual can get into a high-handed kind of situation without the fear of being brought to account or can just keep on acting unjustly.

Is this then a baron's case? No, not any bit.

The Chief Baron of Exchequer is a senior judicial post in the year 1580 in England in the English legal system.

According to Manwood, who was the Chief Baron, in his opinion in the year 1658, considering a touching cooperation, a corporation was invisible, immortal and they hathe no soule and therefore no subpoena lieth against them, because they have no soul or conscience.

In India, during the year 1815, an individual by the name of John Pynder lived who was a critique of certain religious practices followed in the country and he expressed his theological views through his works, Christianity in India (1813) and a Brief account of Jesuits (1815) and Popery, the religion of Heathenian.

In 1820, he as in J Pynder opinionated in his literary extracts that the corporations have no bodies to be punished.

So most everybody felt during those days that Corporations or Companies or LLC (Limited Liability Companies) or the fictitious person from them in the late nineteenth century or the early twentieth century cannot be punished for any atrocities done.

But wait, companies do atrocities during those days? Yes? That is definitely an investigative topic and not a research topic, altogether; but here we must listen to what the literary elites from those days thought about it. So, we may still go on.

Another grandeur, Vincent Stuckey Lean who was an English solicitor and bibliophile made significant proverbs in Collectanea his works, in England. He as in VS Lean thought nothing about the company but everything about administration and he was in full agreement of the proverb, What Lancashire thinks today, all of England will think to-morrow.

Is it not true? No ideas.

Anyway, since then, it is commonly believed that the political movements in Britain always started from Brimingham.

<u>What Manchester says today,...</u>
In 1979, St. Paul's Cathedral in London underwent significant makeover and restoration work where its dome was re-casted and this project was part of a wider and broader 40 million pounds restoration effort that was

started a decade ago preserving the historical grandeur and the Cathedral's structural integrity.

For the benefit of those occasional readers of bibliography, St. Paul's Cathedral is a famous Anglican church and is the seat of the Bishop of London and very much serves the Diocese of London. It is a working church with daily services and prayers, the tradition dating back for more than 1400 years. The main architect of this cathedral after its restoration in the 18th century since it was destroyed by the Great Fire of London in 1666 which destroyed the medieval cathedral was Sir Christopher Wren.

On 24th August 1979, Manchester was at the centre of a significant motorsport event where Ford Cortina, Britain's favourite car entered with a revised model, a generation new of its 1976 model.

A day later on 25th August 1979, bells rang at St Paul's Cathedral to commemorate the wedding of Prince Charles and Lady Diana which was a significant National Event for the UK symbolizing peace, joy, and national unity.

In 1979, Collin Milburn, a notable figure, a cricketer who played for Northamptonshire, who had also lost sight in his one eye owe to a car accident, recorded in his Diaries column, that, Manchester rang its bells yesterday – a day before at St. Paul's, those in justification of his words.

10

Sell side street hawks

It is ironic bantering on difficult tasks that one undertakes be it at a magnitude of space travel or be it fulfilling a porter's job of bearing tremendous and ardent payloads where the premises of work seemingly light weight and the environmental impacts at high risks.

Now, it is heard that the hardworking space agents and explorers are ready to embark on their next flight and fleet and that keeps one guessing what is the motivating factor for all these space travel gimmicks?

Space exploration as a technology and technique has come a long way especially in the wake of space exploration programs design to carry human payloads to Mars, with Elon Musk's SpaceX programs said to have surpassed NASA in certainly in the frequency of space missions undertaken to the ISS International space station alone in recent years.

It is also commendable to hear from experts in Yale University, highlighting the need to build a space ecosystem and an economic task force with missions fulfilling social objectives in space concerning human-rehabilitation, tourism in outer-space mission in order to regain some lost ground for the universities themselves, considering the recent developments in the field.

Remember while going opinionated on this subject, universities like Yale must be taken into confidence especially when it is believed that they are frugally impacted at least financially in the wake of reduced federal funding, crippling or incapacitating their own capacity to do research initiatives in any direction.

But what is spoken about by the same experts is getting venture capital funding for a slew of initiatives concerning space exploration activities just as what happened in the Y2K boom periods for software companies, with a belief that it will start economic activities around setting up businesses or companies fulfilling space launches, merchandises for exploratory tools including software, space insurance services and what not, with the primary aim to expand the tourist map to outer space.

Think about it...

Venture Capital funding used to be a big deal in the early days of year 2000 and it was supposed to initiate seed capital to firms which operated on earth with a feasible but a highly leveraged business idea propelling business transactions that should surpass the level of funding received in tangible terms.

In own experience, while trying to set up a firm in Silicon Valley those days, the idea was to have launched a marketplace for Palm Handheld based software, the firm tasked with development of palm-based utility applications to be showcased later on this marketplace …

The risks in those cases were minimal, either your software marketplace worked, or it does not. If it worked and if you are relatively successful, may be a company like Palm Inc may buy you out partially or fully fulfilling the obligations that you set out with being a borrower in the Venture Capital business or the Angel funding initiatives.

But think about the proposition in space exploration business, here you are talking about human payload, now you cannot even think about your business process going faulty, the risk skyrockets, and it is after considering the risk factors is an extremely dangerous business scenario.

So, before being driven on the buy side street hawk mindset, one must be viciously wise to gauge business propositions that may arise out of such space ventures, driving venture capitalist funding to private but small enterprise offering is not the way ahead, rather the bets are dealt well if it is still be an initiative driven by megalopolis corporate or be fed well by the federal outfits.

<u>Historical leniency and a Heywood</u>
At this onset, it is wise if we say something about John Heywood (1497-1580) who used to live in the year 1546 and as a general observation from few experts, it was told that he did not do well in trade or selling goods through his shops during that time.

Now many refute to say that there are no corroborating evidences to that effect, but most certainly it can be inferred that John Heywood had experienced a penury conceptually while idealising, which is more figurative lament of John rather than a literal one. He may have struggled financially or artistically when on the stage with a patron of marketplace ideas during then.

For the benefit of those ones who seldom forget literary figures, John Heywood is a notable figure from the 16th century. He was an English playwright, musician, and a poet remained active during the reign of Henry VIII, Edward VI, Mary I, and the early Elizabethan reign (Elizabeth I).

Though by profession, he was all that what he was, he was most famous for writing interludes, short comedy plays with themes and political commentaries. He was also well known for his proverbs and his excellent skills that he had, as a poet.

Heywood was a staunch Catholic during a time when there was uprising, upheaval that was significant in the field of religious uprisings in England. His faith was a direct challenge to those with the Monarchs who were Protestants that led his life and career in a more complicated manner, which is evident when one sees that he fled England when England was under Elizabeth I, a Protestant queen.

So, while there is a notion that Heywood was not successful in trade, it is more likely a metaphorical or a reflection of his personal disappointment or a societal satire, as was explained early, rather than a subject of a failed business experience in the modern sense.

Eclogues and Barnabe Googe

The question again on certainly who favoured the fools, and the ordinary, and not the wise, now must be answered, though it is with reverence that one may find amongst the works of a Barnabe Googe, in particular his 1563 work on Eclogues that reflect many proverbs, proverb: Fortune favours fools, is just one among many that he may have had to deal with.

Now about his concerns?

Google laments a sentiment which is reflective of a Renaissance call, a fortune, that is often personified as partially blind and capricious, though he seems to favour the unworthy, the trustworthy, may be trustworthy in the sense in lacking virtue or wisdom, the trust need not be broken, when neglecting the deserved.

In most of his proverb, this paradox is what gets captured suggesting luck is unjust and sometimes arbitrary.

Putting into focus, these idealistic overtures, one can immediately cite that Google always underscored a moral fight and as a result he was in great tension. He apparently dissected social stature and the challenges he faced when observing public attempts at aggrandizing of fortunes were termed and accepted as oriented towards moral murals and meritocracy during those times. His concern was towards the perceived injustice of wise individuals or the so-called enlightened individuals being overlooked and suffering misfortune where the ordinary ones who were less deserving prosper was beyond moral justification, from his standpoint.

The theme under many of his proverbs reflected this with broader Renaissance humanist concerns about unpredictability of fate and of randomness which gave in to more moral implications. He could not but stand the ideals that fools prosper, corrupt gain power and the goods are perished when fresh which were contradictions according to Googe between moralistic desert and actual outcomes which is all part of a persistent philosophical problem, which he tried to solve in a time of religious and political upheaval.

Several others had sentiments quite like him, including Boethius (The Consolation of Philosophy – 6th Century AD), later century writers like Shakespeare (King Lear and Hamlet), and Thomas Wyatt and Henry Howard (Earl of Surrey) expressing frustration in their sonnets with subject: Fortune.

So, Googe's concern is in fact only in line with a personal problem, more a complaint because many did not reflect a broader philosophical disillusionment with the world, in light of which he may have questioned life which seemed to reward flatterers and fools, while those who strive or are strive-errs ignored, questioned, or punished at will during the 16th century.

<u>Gay Fables and fools also err</u>
Another observation lies now and goes, Gay Fables says it is an error that fortune favours fools and wants an immediate answer on the erroneous part, regarding fools and fortunes.

Absolutely yes, In John Gay's Fable XII, Pan and Fortune (1727), the notion of fortune favours fools is challenged presenting a nuanced perspective on merit and luck.

In this fable, Pan who is the god of nature, laments Deciduous forests and its destruction brought about by gamblers, attributing the destruction and hence the devastation on the capriciousness of the Fortune (god). He accuses her of favouring the foolish and of causing ruin. However, Fortune overhears Pan's complaints and responds to him letting him know that she is not 'to blame. She explains many gamblers are knaves who manipulate only some individuals win by chance. Fortune again says and asserts that it is folly, not her, that in most times lead to misfortune.

Another observation regarding deforestation.

Decimating forest leads to afforestation in the long run since in that place something else emerges is quite an ordinary observation. When you fell one tree you make sure 10 trees are planted is another way to look at it.

However, the gigantic trees make it into a thick forest and then the foliage may again prompt more efforts on conservation efforts, wild animal control, capricious beast attacks, and most of what we are up against. That is another take altogether. Let us worry about them later.

So, to interpret Gay, His Fable XII is used by him to critique the misconception that luck is solely the responsibility for success or failure. By personification of Fortune, he contrasted her actions with those of the gamblers. In essence, Gay stresses the universal truth that personal choices and actions play a more deliberate role in outcomes that may follow which may be what is suggested by Gay when he supports the view that attributing one's misfortunes to external forces like luck is a poor decision or is an excuse for one's own folly.

E Phillpotts when he is at Red Redmagnes
Here also, E Phillpotts Oppenheim presents a character whose apparent stupidity leads him to success, where it is told to us that protagonist's lack of intelligence becomes an asset, as it follows him to come out of unexpected situations and to navigate situations with unexpected outcomes, highlighting fortunes and its unpredictable nature.

Olivia Manning and her work, The Great Fortune
Olivia Manning's work The Great Fortune (1960) is her first novel in her Balkan Trilogy, which explores the complexity of human relationships and about fortune and its unpredictable behaviour.

Manning's portrayal of the characters suggests that fortune is not merely a matter of chance but is intricately linked to individual actions and perceptions. For instance, Guy's selflessness and openness to others lead him to form meaningful connections, while Harriet's introspection and scepticism create barriers that isolate her. These dynamics illustrate how personal dispositions can influence one's experience of fortune.

Additionally, the novel's setting during a time of political upheaval underscores the theme that external events can dramatically alter the course of individuals' lives, regardless of their actions. This interplay between personal agency and uncontrollable circumstances reflects the complex nature of fortune and its impact on human lives.

However, *The Great Fortune* delves into themes of uncertainty, displacement, and the complexities of human relationships during the early stages of World War II. The characters, particularly Guy and Harriet Pringle, navigate a world where external events often dictate the pace and direction of their lives. Their experiences in Bucharest, amidst the looming threat of war, reflect a sense of waiting and adaptation to circumstances beyond their control.

In some sense, Mannings original thought, "We were forced to tarry or may be wait while he slumbered or slept" resonates well with Harriet's disposition inspite of her conjugal arrangements with Guy but her confused state of mind gives her allegiance or proximity to Clarence and what about Yakimov? Overall, nothing can be stated about Harriet, only fortunes may have favoured fools, is a very easy predicament, which may have come out of Mannings work.

Avenues to sell and the obstacles

Sell in May and go away, is not a bemusement adage but a carefully followed convention by very old literary figures, a proverb that many may wonder from where those were found, and from when those avenues were open, by preparing to sell junk bonds in Financial Markets, and the right time is all what they were trying hard to find and go with.

Now you may ask who are they?

They are the ones as in the oldest literary figures from English language and from other languages as well.

So, some avenues exist to sell their works; for these very old literary figures, and even then, few chances were always there in the past which they may have used to sell their works...

First, in the year 1979, on 4th May the Daily Telegraph reported that the FT 30 fell 97 points with no immediate relief at sight. What was the cause? Why was it darn opportunistic?

The sharp 97-point drop in the FT30 index in the UK Markets, was part of a broader financial downturn that went on affecting global markets towards the start of the 1970s. This period or the decade long period was marked by several factors which were interrelated contributed to the UK market decline, owe more to 1973-74 Stock Market crash, Stagflation, and a political uncertainty.

The stock market crash of 1973 was triggered by the collapse of Bretton Wood system, Nixon Shock, and the 1973 oil crises which lead to a prolonged bear market for the UK Markets.

Stagflation was a combination of stagnant economic growth, high inflation, which was rising eroding purchase power, economic growth, only aiding investor pessimism.

Finally, there were some political uncertainties, with the Conservative party winning the general election on May3 1979, bringing Margaret Thatcher to power.

Now getting back to the topic: Avenues to sell...

The next chance, was when the Economist in the year, 1992, reported that there was a mention of a month, June, a sluggish period for world stock markets followed by a worse July for the UK Markets.

Yes, there was a global market turmoil in June 1992 in the UK. Many might ask, whether it was because of the Indian economy that was liberalised during that time frame. The short answer to that is, it is not the case. If the Indian markets do well, naturally the UK Markets reflect that.

To say, India's liberalization in 1991 was a positive development for the Global markets, especially the emerging economies. It in fact did not cause the UK or the world market to decline but it was mostly driven by the European monetary instability and the domestic instabilities in the UK.

Primarily it was the result of European currency instability, recession fears in the UK, Global risk aversion and volatile bond markets, in addition to the interest rate shocks which the UK was trying hard to defend.

To get back to our topic, there was again another chance to sell junk bonds this time based on a report from New York Times that the dot com which was a big thing towards the beginning of the millennium, bust. The report was that there was a pattern of stock market fluctuations particularly in the Information Technology sector and the period was marked by the bursting of dot-com bubble which impacted the global financial markets. The report also magnified the relevance of this quote: Sell in May, and come back on St. Leger's Day; to mention a well-known piece of market folklore suggesting investors should sell the normal stock in May and refrain from entering the market until September, which coincided with the St. Leger Stakes, a classical horse race of the British flat racing season. However, it was a perfect opportunity to sell junk bonds, by anticipating a raise in shortlisting firms who performed worst in the current season.

The quote and the Aftermath for the Commoner

In 2002, The New York Times referenced the quote: Sell in May, and come back on St. Leger's Day by saying in the context of market behaviour during the early 2000s. At that time, the U.S. stock market was experiencing significant volatility, influenced by factors such as the burst of the dot-com bubble, and the aftermath of the September 11 attacks.

Many fell, stock markets crashed, many could not comprehend the idealistic favouritism that was in existence until then, totally changed. There were frugal economic conditions, horrible market sentiments, and geopolitical events that unravelled and hence the investors were advised by experts to exercise caution and consider a comprehensive analysis before making investment decisions based on these seasonal adages or proverbs, considering well that it benefits a who and devastates a clerihew.

In actual essentials, in the English literature, literals rule and literature follow through, the markets benefit whether it is a fall or a rise, whether it is bull or a bear and it is wise not to be bothered for orders based on old adages; there are literary figures who are immortal, in English and in very many languages. To reiterate, let us not be bothered about proverbs or adages. Let the literary figures do their selling, the adages go on, as it has gone on for ages.